Original title:
Happy Vibes

Copyright © 2024 Creative Arts Management OÜ
All rights reserved.

Author: Thor Castlebury
ISBN HARDBACK: 978-9916-88-208-5
ISBN PAPERBACK: 978-9916-88-209-2

**Glistening & Grinning**

Sunlight dances on the stream,
Laughter echoes, soft as cream.
Shining faces in the glow,
Joyful hearts, we ebb and flow.

A gentle breeze whispers low,
Whirled around in nature's show.
Glistening dreams, bright and free,
Grinning wide, just you and me.

**Sparkling Moments**

Stars ignite the velvet sky,
Moments twinkle, drifting by.
A sudden smile, a knowing glance,
In the night, we take a chance.

Soft whispers, secrets shared,
In the magic, we are bared.
Sparkling memories interlace,
In the warmth of this embrace.

**Festive Footprints in the Sand**

Waves lap gently at the shore,
Joyful laughter, we want more.
Footprints left where tides embrace,
Memories made, in this safe space.

Underneath the sun's bright glow,
Festive hearts begin to flow.
Sandcastles rise, dreams take flight,
Footprints fade into the night.

## Cheerful Little Secrets

In the garden, whispers bloom,
Secrets twirl, dispelling gloom.
Petals soft beneath our feet,
Hidden joys in moments sweet.

Laughter dances on the breeze,
Time stands still with such ease.
Cheerful wonders in our hearts,
In the light, our friendship starts.

## Sweet Sips of Bliss

In the morning light, a cup of cheer,
Warmth in my hands, the world feels near.
Hints of cinnamon dance in the air,
Each sip a moment, nothing to spare.

Clouds drift by, soft in their grace,
Nature's beauty, a calming embrace.
Joy found in flavors, rich and divine,
In every sweet drop, I savor the time.

## The Energy of Enthusiasm

A spark ignites in the depths of the soul,
Fueling the fire, making us whole.
With every heartbeat, passion takes flight,
Chasing our dreams, into the night.

Voices lift high, in harmony sing,
Together we rise, oh, what joy we bring.
With each burst of laughter, spirits align,
Unstoppable force, a vision divine.

**Vivid Moments**

Captured in frames, colors collide,
Memories painted, with love as the guide.
Whispers of laughter, echoes of cheer,
In vivid snapshots, we hold what is dear.

Each glance a reminder, of times we embraced,
In the tapestry woven, no moment erased.
Life's fleeting treasures, like starlight they gleam,
In the heart's gallery, we chase every dream.

**The Pulse of Joy**

Feel the rhythm, a soft embrace,
Joy's gentle pulse, in every space.
With open hearts, let laughter flow,
In unity's dance, we endlessly glow.

Moments of wonder, like sunbeams they play,
Life's simple pleasures, in bright hues array.
Together we thrive, in joy we unite,
The essence of happiness, our guiding light.

## Uplifting Serenades

In the dawn's soft embrace,
Hope sings a gentle tune.
Whispers of joy in the air,
Hearts dance beneath the moon.

Gentle breezes carry tales,
Of love and laughter anew.
Each moment a precious gift,
Together, we'll break through.

Sunlight bathes the fields bright,
Colors bloom with pure delight.
Every step feels like a song,
Guided by the stars' light.

With every heartbeat we share,
The world feels lighter still.
Together in this melody,
We find our strength and will.

# **Glimmers of Bliss**

In quiet corners of the day,
Glimmers sparkle like the stars.
Moments woven soft and bright,
Healing all of life's scars.

Laughter dances on the breeze,
Joy bubbles in the streams.
Chasing shadows with warm light,
We awaken from our dreams.

Nature sings a symphony,
Each note a sweet caress.
Together in this harmony,
We find our happiness.

Hearts united, spirits soar,
In every gentle glance.
With every breath, we find more,
In life's eternal dance.

# **Breaths of Elation**

In the stillness of the morn,
Breaths of elation rise high.
With each pulse, new hopes are born,
In the vast and open sky.

Moments caught between the waves,
Whispers carried by the sea.
In the rhythm, courage paves,
Paths to who we're meant to be.

Flowers bloom in sunlight's gaze,
Painting life with vibrant hue.
With each footstep, joy displays,
All the beauty felt so true.

Glimpses of a brighter day,
Dance like shadows in the light.
In every heartbeat, come what may,
We embrace the world with delight.

## The Pursuit of Joy

In the journey of our lives,
We seek the stars that shine bright.
With every laugh, hope survives,
   Turning darkness into light.

Dreams like butterflies take flight,
Chasing moments filled with grace.
In the pursuit, we ignite,
   Wonders time cannot erase.

Together we will explore,
Paths where happiness unfolds.
Every step, we find much more,
A tale of love that never holds.

With open hearts, we shall roam,
Into the wild, vast expanse.
In this pursuit, we find home,
A dance where souls take their chance.

**Waves of Warmth**

The sun sets low, a golden hue,
Soft whispers carried by the blue.
Gentle tides lap at the shore,
Embracing all, forevermore.

A tranquil breeze, a sweet caress,
Nature's warmth, we must confess.
Hearts expand like ocean's swell,
In this peace, we find our dwell.

Children laugh, their voices blend,
In waves of warmth, all troubles mend.
A moment shared, a smile bright,
Together we bask in fading light.

As twilight calls, the stars ignite,
Waves of warmth, a pure delight.
Connected souls, hand in hand,
We ride the tides, we understand.

## The Song of Simplicity

A leaf floats down, a soft embrace,
The world turns slow, a gentle pace.
In the quiet, we hear it call,
The song of life, it sings to all.

Moments shared, a fleeting glance,
In simple joys, we find our chance.
A child's laughter, a lover's sigh,
In these small things, we learn to fly.

Worn-out paths, yet still we roam,
In simplicity, we find our home.
A cup of tea, a cozy nook,
Life's greatest treasures in every book.

So let us dance to this sweet refrain,
In the song of simplicity, we gain.
Each heartbeat sings, each breath a gift,
In this melody, our spirits lift.

# Cheerful Horizons

Morning breaks with colors bright,
Brushstrokes of joy, a pure delight.
As daylight beams upon our way,
Cheerful horizons beckon today.

Birds in flight, they sing their tune,
Chasing dreams, they soar and swoon.
A heart full of hope, a light embrace,
Cheerful horizons fill the space.

Laughter echoes through the air,
With every step, we walk with care.
The world alive with gleeful sights,
In each small moment, pure delight.

Hold on tight to love's embrace,
Cheerful horizons, a vibrant place.
Together we rise, hand in hand,
Painting the skies with dreams so grand.

## **Whirlwind of Positivity**

A storm of smiles, a vivid burst,
In every heart, the joy can thirst.
With open arms, we greet the tide,
Whirlwind of positivity, our guide.

Kind words ripple, soft and true,
They grow like flowers, fresh with dew.
In the chaos, find your space,
Embrace the light, find your place.

Laughter dances, pure and free,
In this whirlwind, we are we.
Hope is found in every glance,
Together we sway, a joyful dance.

So let us spin in this bright gale,
Whirlwind of positivity will not fail.
With every heartbeat, let love flow,
In this vast world, let kindness grow.

## Sunshine's Embrace

Golden rays touch the earth,
Whispers of warmth give birth.
Gentle breezes softly play,
Every moment, bright as day.

Fields of gold stretch afar,
Chasing dreams like a star.
Nature's glow, a sweet delight,
Filling hearts with pure light.

In the glow, laughter beams,
Hope entwined in sunny dreams.
With each dawn, fresh starts arise,
Underneath the endless skies.

Sunshine paints the world anew,
Every hue a vibrant view.
With love's warmth, we find our way,
In sunshine's embrace, we stay.

## **Sparkling Inspirations**

Glimmers dance upon the sea,
Ideas flow wild and free.
Moments caught in fleeting flight,
Inspiration shines so bright.

Stars that twinkle in the night,
Kindling thoughts, igniting light.
Words that spark, a gentle fire,
Filling hearts with sweet desire.

Dreams that soar, like birds in air,
Follow them, if you dare.
Life's a canvas, brush in hand,
Create, explore, just take a stand.

In the spark, we find our place,
Each idea, a warm embrace.
With hope lighting our way,
Sparkling inspirations sway.

## **Elysian Fields of Laughter**

Rolling hills, a bright expanse,
Where joy invites us to dance.
Echoes of laughter fill the air,
In this place, we shed our care.

Flowers bloom in colors bold,
Stories whispered, tales retold.
Joyful hearts in unity,
Elysian fields are wild and free.

Children playing, spirits bright,
Chasing dreams from day to night.
Laughter rings as friendships grow,
In fields where purest love can flow.

With each smile, the world we mend,
In laughter's arms, we transcend.
Here's to joy that's ever near,
Elysian fields draw us near.

**Journeys of Joy**

Paths unknown stretch wide ahead,
With open hearts, we're gently led.
Every step a chance to find,
Joy that soothes the wandering mind.

Mountains high and rivers clear,
Glimpses of wonder draw us near.
With each turn, the world unfolds,
Journeys filled with magic told.

Friends beside, hand in hand,
Together in this wondrous land.
Memories made in every glance,
In laughter, we forever dance.

Chasing sunsets, wide and bright,
Journeys lead us to the light.
With each moment, hearts deploy,
In the beauty of our joy.

## The Canvas of Joy

Bright colors splash on white,
Each stroke a laugh, a light.
Laughter dances on the page,
Joy painted in every stage.

Moments captured, pure and free,
A gallery of memory.
Each hue a story, each brush a song,
In this place where we belong.

Together we create and dream,
Life's canvas, a flowing stream.
With hands intertwined, we start,
Painting joy straight from the heart.

## Sun-kissed Memories

Golden rays on soft skin,
Memories where joy begins.
Laughter echoes in warm air,
Moments cherished, none to spare.

Footprints tracing on warm sand,
Holding tight, a loving hand.
Sunsets paint the sky aglow,
In this warmth, our spirits flow.

Days pass swift, like fleeting light,
Sun-kissed dreams in gentle night.
Remembered whispers, sweet embrace,
In every heart, a sacred space.

## A Whiff of Delight

Sweet scent of blooms in spring,
Nature's gifts, the joy they bring.
A soft breeze carries the sound,
Of laughter in the garden found.

Candied dreams and sugar skies,
Tickling noses, sweet surprise.
Each breath a burst of bliss,
In this moment, what we miss.

Lemonade on sunny days,
Memories wrapped in sunny rays.
Every flavor, every taste,
In the heart, no joy can waste.

# **Twinkling Eyes and Sunshine**

Her laughter rings like chimes,
In the warmth of playful times.
Twinkling eyes, a playful glance,
Inviting joy, a sweet romance.

Sunshine threads through every smile,
Lighting up each precious mile.
Moments captured, pure delight,
In the sparkle, hearts take flight.

Under skies of azure blue,
Every day feels fresh and new.
Each twinkle tells a story bright,
In the warmth of love's pure light.

**Dancing on Cloud Nine**

In the sky, we twirl and spin,
With laughter that dances on the wind.
Soft whispers float through the air,
Each moment a treasure, beyond compare.

Cotton candy dreams align,
Beneath the stars, we intertwine.
Floating high, hearts full of cheer,
In this bliss, we lose all fear.

## Vibrant Heartbeats

Colors burst with every beat,
As rhythms move the dancing feet.
A harmony of joy and light,
In every pulse, our spirits unite.

Whispers of life, bold and bright,
Echoing softly in the night.
Together we create a song,
In this world, where we belong.

**Daydreams in Bloom**

Petals unfurl in the golden sun,
Each daydream whispers, 'You've just begun.'
In gardens where hopes come alive,
We plant our wishes, we learn to thrive.

Butterflies dance as visions soar,
In fragrant moments, we seek for more.
A tapestry woven with colors bright,
In the tapestry of day and night.

## A Symphony of Smiles

Joy resonates in the heart's embrace,
Notes of laughter fill the space.
With every smile, a story told,
In this symphony, warmth unfolds.

Together we weave a melody sweet,
In the rhythm of life, our hearts meet.
With every glance, our spirits rise,
In the harmony of love, we realize.

## Joyful Whispers of the Heart

In the quiet of the morning,
A soft breeze stirs the leaves.
Whispers of happiness echo,
Carried on gentle dreams.

Laughter dances on the air,
As sunlight paints the skies.
Every heartbeat sings a tune,
Love's melody never dies.

Moments cherished, held so dear,
In memories wrapped so tight.
Joy flows freely, pure and bright,
Guiding souls through day and night.

With every step, the heart leaps,
In the rhythm of the now.
Embrace the whispers of the heart,
As time takes a gentle bow.

**Radiant Moments**

Golden rays touch the earth,
Painting scenes with warm delight.
Time slows down in wondrous birth,
As day bids farewell to night.

In every smile, a story blooms,
In laughter, echoes rise and fall.
The heart finds peace amidst the glooms,
In radiant moments, we stand tall.

Dreams glimmer like distant stars,
Whispers float on evening air.
Together, we heal our scars,
In love's embrace, we are aware.

The world is full of gentle grace,
Each heartbeat a precious thread.
In every moment, we find our place,
Where joy and hope are gently fed.

## Blissful Echoes

In the forest deep and wide,
Nature hums a soft refrain.
Every breeze is a joyful guide,
Leading hearts to peace again.

The river sings its timeless tune,
As shadows dance beneath the trees.
Each note drifts like a silver moon,
Whispering promises with ease.

In sunsets painted shades of gold,
The heart finds solace, soft and sweet.
Stories of love and life retold,
In echoes where our souls do meet.

With every moment flowing free,
We embrace the blissful calling.
Together, as one, we shall be,
In echoes of joy, forever enthralling.

## Dance of the Fireflies

In the evening's gentle glow,
Fireflies sparkle, light the night.
They weave a dance, soft and slow,
Guiding dreams with their bright flight.

With every flicker, a tale is spun,
Of magic hidden in the dark.
The world awakens, shadows run,
As the stars put on their spark.

Whispers of love in the cool, calm air,
Entwined in movements, soft and shy.
We twirl beneath the moon's sweet care,
In the dance of the fireflies, we sigh.

As night wraps us in its embrace,
We find our rhythm, hearts aligned.
In this enchanting, twinkling space,
The dance of life, beautifully designed.

## **Sparkle in Your Step**

With every stride, you light the way,
A twinkle shines in the words you say.
Your laughter dances on the breeze,
Bringing joy that flows with ease.

Each moment glimmers like a star,
In the night sky, you've come so far.
With a sparkle bright, you leap and twirl,
Creating magic in this world.

Every glance, a radiant glow,
Like morning dew on flowers that grow.
You tread on dreams, both bold and bright,
Igniting paths with pure delight.

So keep that sparkle, let it beam,
A friend like you fulfills the dream.
In every heart, you leave a trace,
A cherished glow, a warm embrace.

## **A Garden of Giggles**

In a garden where laughter blooms,
Joyful echoes fill the rooms.
Petals dance with playful grace,
Smiles infuse this happy space.

Sunlight dapples through the trees,
Whispers carried by the breeze.
Each giggle sprouts like tender shoots,
Growing joy in playful roots.

Bumblebees hum, butterflies glide,
With every giggle, hearts collide.
Nature smiles, as we delight,
In this garden, pure and bright.

So come and laugh, let worries cease,
In this garden, find your peace.
With every chuckle, dreams take flight,
Creating memories that feel just right.

## The Sunshine Within

Deep inside, a light does gleam,
A gentle warmth, a quiet dream.
With hope ablaze in every heart,
We shine together, never apart.

When shadows fall and doubts arise,
Look within, to see the skies.
The sunshine glows, bright and clear,
In every moment, it is near.

Let kindness be the guiding spark,
A beacon shining in the dark.
With every smile, let love begin,
And find the sunshine deep within.

So radiate, let spirits soar,
With each bright pulse, we're evermore.
Embrace the warmth, let worries thin,
And cherish all the light within.

## **Radiance of Togetherness**

Hands held tight, we journey far,
With shared dreams, we shine like stars.
In every laugh, in every tear,
Together, we conquer every fear.

Through the storms, our bond stays strong,
In unity, we always belong.
Each heartbeat echoes, strong and true,
A symphony of me and you.

In quiet moments, joy unfolds,
In stories shared, and hands we hold.
The light we share, a guiding thread,
In togetherness, our hearts are fed.

So here's to us, forever bright,
Embracing love, a wondrous sight.
In every challenge, let's stand tall,
Together, we can conquer all.

## **Smiles in the Meadow**

In the meadow green and wide,
Where petals dance with joy inside,
Children laugh and run around,
In this place, pure bliss is found.

Breezes whisper through the grass,
Tickling toes as moments pass,
Daisies bloom with faces bright,
Underneath the warm sunlight.

Each breath a sweet and gentle sigh,
Nature's beauty draws us nigh,
With every smile shared today,
In the meadow, hearts will stay.

## The Art of Lightness

Floating like a feather's tune,
Beneath the silver crescent moon,
Life's burdens softly released,
In the dance, our souls are pleased.

Whispers of the evening breeze,
Caress the spirit, aim to please,
With every step, we rise and sway,
Finding joy in simple play.

Laughter echoes through the night,
As we embrace the pure delight,
In a canvas painted bright,
The art of lightness takes its flight.

## Uplifted Spirits

In the morning's golden glow,
Hearts awaken, feelings flow,
With hope rising in the air,
Uplifted spirits, light to share.

Every dream that dares to climb,
Finds its rhythm, adds to rhyme,
With every step, we elevate,
Together forging brighter fate.

Side by side, we bridge the gap,
Filling spaces like a map,
A tapestry of joy and grace,
Uplifted spirits find their place.

## **Cherished Sunbeams**


Golden rays that warm the skin,
In their glow, our dreams begin,
Every moment, bright and clear,
Cherished sunbeams drawing near.

Through the branches, light will play,
Painting shadows in array,
Nature whispers, soft and warm,
In the light, we find our charm.

With open eyes, we greet the day,
Embracing joy in every way,
Together basking in the streams,
Of cherished sunbeams, hopes, and dreams.

## **Heartfelt Revelries**

In shadows cast by twilight glow,
Whispers of dreams begin to flow.
Hearts entwined in soft embrace,
Memories linger, a tender trace.

Laughter dances, merry and light,
Chasing away the depths of night.
Under stars, our secrets shared,
In these moments, we felt prepared.

With every cheer, our spirits rise,
Together we soar, beneath the skies.
In heartfelt revelries, we sing,
Cherishing the joy that moments bring.

## **A Tapestry of Chimes**

Bells ring softly in the breeze,
A melody that softly frees.
Threads of sound weave through the air,
Crafting stories, pure and fair.

Each note a color, bright and bold,
A tapestry of dreams untold.
In the rhythm, we find our peace,
As all our worries start to cease.

Chimes resound in the quiet night,
Guiding us with gentle light.
In this harmony, hearts entwine,
A song of love, pure and divine.

## **Sunrise Serenade**

With dawn's embrace, the world awakes,
Golden rays, a gift that breaks.
Nature sings as shadows flee,
In the light, we feel so free.

Birds take flight on morning wings,
Chirping bright, the joy it brings.
A serenade of colors rise,
Painting warmth across the skies.

Together, we greet the new day,
In its magic, we long to stay.
Sunrise whispers, soft and sweet,
Life's new chapters, an endless beat.

## **Laughter in the Breeze**

Laughter echoes through the trees,
Carried gently on the breeze.
Joyful hearts, a playful sound,
In these moments, peace is found.

Children's giggles, pure delight,
Chasing shadows, hearts so light.
In every chuckle, a spark ignites,
Illuminating our starry nights.

With every laugh, the world feels bright,
Together we stand, hearts alight.
In laughter's dance, we find our place,
Wrapping us in a warm embrace.

## Radiance in Every Step


With every step, a glow does rise,
A spark of light that fills the skies.
Each moment shines, a dance of grace,
A journey bright, we all embrace.

Through shadows cast, we find our way,
In laughter shared, at break of day.
Hearts alight on paths we tread,
A trail of peace, where dreams are spread.

Each whispering breeze, a gentle guide,
Illuminates where hope resides.
With faith as strong as morning sun,
Together we walk, forever one.

**Garden of Giggles**

In a garden where laughter blooms,
Joyful echoes chase away glooms.
Petals dance with a playful sway,
In the sunlight, come out to play.

Bubbles float on the breeze so sweet,
Chasing sunshine on little feet.
Each giggle sprouts like flowers bright,
Making every soul feel light.

Underneath the azure skies,
Children's laughter, a sweet surprise.
In this haven where dreams do weave,
We find magic, we believe.

**Elation's Canvas**

On a canvas bright, emotions blend,
Swirls of color, joy transcends.
Brushstrokes weave tales of delight,
Crafting visions, pure and bright.

Each hue reflects a heart's own song,
With every detail, vibrant and strong.
In this gallery of dreams and hopes,
Imagination gives us ropes.

The laughter mingles with shades of gold,
Stories of wonder waiting to be told.
In art's embrace, we learn to see,
The pure elation of being free.

## Sunrise of Serenity

As dawn unfolds, a gentle light,
Painting skies with hues so bright.
In stillness, nature finds its grace,
A quiet moment, a soft embrace.

The world awakens, calm and clear,
Whispers of peace drift ever near.
With every breath, our souls align,
In this dawn, we feel divine.

Birdsongs weave through air so sweet,
Harmony sings, a rhythmic beat.
In the warmth of the sun's first glow,
Serenity whispers, 'Let love flow.'

## Uplifted Spirits

In the morning glow of dawn,
Hope rises with the sun's warm song.
Hearts lifted high, we find our way,
Together we'll dance, come what may.

Breezes whisper tales of cheer,
Each moment precious, drawing near.
With laughter bright, our worries fade,
In this journey, love won't evade.

Through valleys low and mountains steep,
We'll hold each other, promises keep.
Uplifted spirits, we stand tall,
United in joy, we'll never fall.

With every step, the world is wide,
In our hearts, we let love guide.
Embrace the magic that we share,
In uplifted spirits, free as air.

## **Kaleidoscope of Delight**

Colors swirling in the air,
A vibrant dance, beyond compare.
Moments bright, they intertwine,
In this kaleidoscope, you are mine.

Every shadow finds its light,
In the laughter, spirits ignite.
Each hue whispers stories past,
In this pattern, dreams are cast.

Twinkling stars in the velvet night,
Reflect our joy, a timeless sight.
With every glance, our hearts align,
In this kaleidoscope, love's design.

Let us twirl, let laughter ring,
In this dance, our souls will sing.
A tapestry of smiles we weave,
In this delight, we truly believe.

## Embracing the Light

As shadows fade and dawn awakes,
We find the strength that hope creates.
With open arms, we greet the day,
Embracing light along the way.

Through storms we've walked, hand in hand,
Our hearts are strong, together we stand.
In the warmth of love, fears take flight,
With every heartbeat, we embrace the light.

Moments cherished, memories bright,
We walk with purpose, eyes in sight.
No darkness can our dreams outshine,
As we embrace this love divine.

Through every trial, we will rise,
With faith that shines, like endless skies.
Embracing the light, we'll take our flight,
Together always, hearts burning bright.

# **Chirping Melodies**

In the grove where birdies play,
Chirping melodies greet the day.
Each note a whisper of the trees,
A symphony carried on the breeze.

Nature's song fills the morning light,
Laughing leaves in pure delight.
With vibrant chirps, the world awakes,
In harmony, our spirit breaks.

Fluttering wings and joyous calls,
In this moment, peace enthralls.
With every chirp, our worries cease,
In nature's embrace, we find our peace.

So let us cherish this sweet refrain,
In the heart of spring, love will remain.
As melodies dance through the air,
We join the song, free from despair.

### **Echoes of Laughter**

In the quiet of the night,
Laughter dances on the breeze,
Whispers of the past take flight,
With memories that never cease.

Joyful echoes fill the air,
Softly ringing through the gloom,
Each note a reminder, rare,
Of how we always find our room.

Moments shared, a brilliant spark,
Lighting up the shadowed way,
Together we ignite the dark,
Creating warmth where hearts can play.

So let us laugh beneath the stars,
And treasure every fleeting sound,
For in each smile, no matter how far,
The beauty of our bond is found.

## The Brightness of Being

In the morning's gentle light,
Hope awakens with the dawn,
Each breath a chance to feel so right,
A canvas blank to draw upon.

Colors splash across the day,
With dreams that soar on silver wings,
In every step, we find our way,
Embracing all the joy life brings.

Moments fleeting, yet so sweet,
In laughter shared, our spirits grow,
Together, every heart can beat,
In the dance of life, we'll glow.

So let your light shine bright and free,
For in your heart, treasures lie,
The brightness of just being me,
Is a gift that will never die.

## **Kaleidoscope of Cheer**

Colors swirl in joyous play,
Each turn reveals a new delight,
In every glance, a chance to say,
Life is vibrant, pure, and bright.

Laughter bubbles like a stream,
Glistening with the morning's ray,
Together weaving every dream,
In a tapestry we display.

With every hug, the warmth we share,
Brings comfort in the darkest night,
In a world beyond compare,
Kaleidoscopes bring pure delight.

So let us twirl in life's embrace,
For every hue will find its tune,
In this dance, we find our place,
A symphony beneath the moon.

# Glowing Conversations

Beneath the stars, we find our way,
Words igniting like the flame,
In every laugh, in every say,
Connections grow, they never wane.

Thoughts like lanterns in the night,
Guiding dreams that softly glow,
In silent whispers, hearts take flight,
Through shared stories, love can flow.

Every word a shining thread,
Weaving magic into space,
In the silence, softly said,
Are the feelings we embrace.

So gather round and speak your truth,
Let your voice be heard so clear,
In the light of hope and youth,
Our glowing conversations near.

## Effervescent Dreams

Bubbles dance in twilight beams,
Whispers float on gentle streams.
Thoughts like stars in velvet air,
Sparkle softly, dreamers share.

Fleeting moments, silver gleam,
Chasing shadows, lost in theme.
Eager hearts with wishful eyes,
Soar on wings, and softly rise.

Hopes ignite like fireflies,
Lighting paths where silence lies.
In the night, our spirits gleam,
Living bright the effervescent dream.

Each heartbeat sings, a vibrant tune,
Underneath the watchful moon.
In this space, we dare to roam,
Finding faith, and making home.

## **Cascade of Smiles**

Tears of joy, like morning dew,
Flowing soft, fresh and new.
Every glance, a glowing light,
Warming hearts with pure delight.

Children laugh, their voices clear,
Echoing for all to hear.
Like a stream that winds and glides,
Happiness in every stride.

Hands entwined through sunlit days,
Sharing love in countless ways.
Gentle kindness, a sweet refrain,
Creating memories, breaking chains.

In the rush of life's embrace,
Smiles cascade, a soft grace.
Groves of hope with every mile,
Living life with a cascade of smiles.

## **Warmth in Every Step**

Walking through the golden light,
Every moment, pure and bright.
Footprints whisper stories old,
Tales of courage, hearts so bold.

Sunrise paints the world in gold,
Glimmers soft, the warmth unfolds.
Hand in hand on paths we tread,
Building dreams, where hopes are bred.

In the chill of evening's fold,
Love's embrace will never grow cold.
Every step, a promise made,
Together strong, we will not fade.

With each stride, the world we mend,
Finding joy around each bend.
Together through the night and day,
Warmth in every step, we sway.

## **Luminescent Journeys**

Stars align on paths we roam,
Guiding us to find our home.
Light cascades through shadowed fears,
Filling hearts with hope and cheers.

Every turn, a story spun,
Chasing dreams, we laugh and run.
Past the mountains, skies so blue,
Find the light that dwells in you.

Through the darkness, courage beams,
Illuminating cherished dreams.
Travel far, but always near,
Whispers of those loved and dear.

In luminescent paths we tread,
Together onward, softly led.
With each journey, new and bright,
We will dance through endless light.

## **Warmth of the Sunlit Path**

Golden rays dance on the ground,
Whispers of nature all around.
Each footstep soft upon the way,
Guided by light of a brightening day.

Trees sway gently in the breeze,
Carrying secrets, giving ease.
The world awakens from its night,
Breathing deeply, hearts feel light.

Beneath the sky's vast, blue expanse,
Life unfolds, a vibrant dance.
Paths may twist, but never stray,
As love and joy show us the way.

Embrace the warmth, feel it grow,
Within our hearts, a radiant glow.
On this sunlit path we tread,
In nature's arms, we're gently led.

## The Color of Cheer

Bright yellow blooms 'neath the sun,
A tapestry of joy begun.
Playful hues that draw a smile,
Jazzing up life, making it worthwhile.

Butterflies dance on petals neat,
With every flutter, life's a treat.
Crimson roses, violet skies,
A canvas where cheer never dies.

Laughter rings in the warm air,
Joy painted everywhere.
Emotions swirling, bold and free,
In this kaleidoscope, we see.

Colors meld, creating art,
Each one a beat, a vibrant part.
Life bursts forth in shades so bright,
The color of cheer, the purest light.

**Blissful Tranquility**

In the stillness, soft and clear,
Peaceful moments draw us near.
The whispering winds in morning light,
A gentle sigh, the world feels right.

Rippling waters kiss the shore,
Nature's lullaby, forevermore.
A quiet heart among the trees,
Finding solace in the breeze.

Mountains stand with grace and pride,
In their shadow, troubles hide.
With every breath, the calm we seek,
In tranquil spaces, hearts can speak.

Stars above in silent song,
In their glow, we belong.
Embracing night with open arms,
In blissful tranquility, life charms.

## **Glistening Moments**

Morning dew on blades of grass,
Whispers of time as moments pass.
Each droplet holds a world within,
Glistening bright, where dreams begin.

Sunset spills a golden hue,
Casting shadows, painting the view.
Every second, a fleeting sight,
Captured gently in warm light.

Waves crash softly on the sand,
Nature's rhythm, steady and grand.
Footprints trace a fleeting dance,
In these glistening moments, take a chance.

Life's mosaic, each piece a gleam,
In every heartbeat, a sparkling dream.
Through time's embrace, we always find,
Glistening moments, sweet and kind.

## **Unwritten Adventures of Joy**

In the whispers of the trees,
Where laughter dances in the breeze,
Moments hidden, waiting to be,
Joy unfolds in wild spree.

Footsteps lead to paths unknown,
With each step, our spirits grown.
Every turn a chance to find,
The stories etched in heart and mind.

Stars above, a guiding light,
In the night, our dreams take flight.
With every heartbeat, joy's embrace,
Unwritten tales in this sacred space.

Let us journey, hand in hand,
Together we will boldly stand.
The canvas bright with colors new,
Adventures waiting just for you.

## Heartwarming Breezes

Gentle winds caress the fields,
Nature's love forever yields.
Warmth of sun on tender skin,
Heartbeats quicken, joy begins.

In the shade where laughter shared,
Every moment freely bared.
Drifting whispers through the trees,
Capturing life's simple keys.

Memories float like petals soft,
Carried high, they lift us off.
Together, we will always be,
Bound by heart, forever free.

In every breeze, let spirits soar,
Finding treasures to explore.
With joy and love, the sweetest song,
Heartwarming breezes where we belong.

## The Glow of Togetherness

In the glow of a setting sun,
Together, our hearts beat as one.
Sharing stories, dreams, and fears,
Laughter mingles with our tears.

Candles flicker, shadows play,
In this moment, night turns to day.
With hands entwined, the world feels right,
Together, we shine, our hearts alight.

The warmth of love, a guiding star,
No distance ever seems too far.
In every hug, a spark ignites,
Togetherness, our greatest rights.

Each glance a promise, a silent vow,
In this life, we choose the how.
With every step, we find our way,
The glow of togetherness will stay.

## The Essence of Cheer

In the morning light so clear,
We find the essence of cheer.
With smiles bright, we greet the day,
Letting joy lead us on our way.

Laughter blooms in every space,
Creating warmth, a soft embrace.
In kind words, our spirits lift,
The beauty found in friendship's gift.

Through seasons change, we'll always share,
Moments bright, beyond compare.
With open hearts and hands outstretched,
The essence of cheer, forever etched.

So let us cherish, hold it tight,
The joy we find, our hearts in flight.
In every moment, let us steer,
Together, we share the essence of cheer.

## A Symphony of Joy

Joy dances on the breeze,
Notes of laughter fill the air,
Children play beneath the trees,
Sunshine wraps us in a care.

Melodies of everyday,
Echoes of a happy song,
Hearts in rhythm as we sway,
Together, we truly belong.

Colors bloom in vibrant light,
Moments weave a joyful thread,
Stars above shine soft and bright,
In this symphony, we're led.

Life's a song, so sweet and clear,
Every note a treasured part,
In this music, we find cheer,
A symphony that warms the heart.

## The Flavor of Laughter

Laughter bubbles like a brook,
Sweetness drips from every sound,
Just like honey, joy's the hook,
In its flavor, we are found.

Brighter days are made to share,
With the spice of playful fun,
In the moments that we dare,
Life becomes a race well-run.

Each giggle adds a pinch of zest,
Lively echoes fill the room,
In this feast, we are the guests,
Savor joy that will not bloom.

Taste the magic in the air,
A recipe for all to know,
With laughter's warmth beyond compare,
Together, we make life glow.

## **Gleeful Adventures Await**

In the dawn, the world awakes,
Promises whispered in the sun,
Every path and step it takes,
Holds a tale of joy begun.

Maps of dreams, we spread them wide,
Hearts are ready, spirits bold,
Through the hills, we're on a ride,
Chasing stories yet untold.

Wonders soft beneath our feet,
In the glades, we laugh and play,
Every moment feels so sweet,
Gleeful adventures lead the way.

Together, we will find the thrill,
In the places yet to roam,
With each step, a joyful fill,
Hand in hand, we make our home.

## **Serendipity in the Air**

Whispers of fate float on high,
In the shimmers of the night,
Chance encounters, sweet as pie,
Bring us joy, and pure delight.

Wandering hearts, we roam so free,
Open arms to greet surprise,
Moments bloom serendipity,
Magic hidden in our eyes.

Every turn holds a new chance,
In the dance of day and fate,
Twisting paths lead us to glance,
At the wonders we create.

So we cherish every find,
Celebrate the gifts we share,
In this journey, we unwind,
Serendipity's in the air.

## **Chasing Rainbows**

In the sky, colors blend bright,
Chasing dreams, a wondrous sight.
Running fast, heart full of cheer,
Hoping to catch what seems so near.

Footprints fade on the grass below,
With every step, a hint of glow.
The laughter echoes, spirits rise,
In every hue, love never lies.

Storms may pass, skies turn gray,
But after the rain, bright lights play.
With patience gained from time's embrace,
We find our bliss in every trace.

Embrace the path, the winding way,
For rainbows bless both dusk and day.
In chasing light, we learn to see,
The treasures of our journey, free.

**The Sweetness of Now**

Moments linger, soft and bright,
In the hush of gentle night.
Savor whispers, laughter shared,
In the present, love declared.

Butterflies dance, time stands still,
In this instant, hearts can fill.
Each breath taken, a treasure found,
In simple joys, the world goes round.

Sunrise colors paint the dawn,
With every tick, a bond is drawn.
Hold on tightly, don't let go,
For the sweet now is what we know.

Days may pass, and seasons change,
Yet memories learned will rearrange.
In living fully, we can see,
The sweetness of now, eternally.

## **Heartfelt Harmonies**

In twilight's glow, voices unite,
Melodies weave through the night.
Strings and keys, emotions flow,
In every note, connection grows.

Hearts entwined in rhythmic beat,
In the silence, love is sweet.
Harmony sings, a gentle kiss,
In music's arms, we find our bliss.

Fingers dance on ivory white,
Creating worlds, pure delight.
With every swell, a story told,
In heartfelt tones, we are consoled.

Let the symphony lift us high,
Underneath the endless sky.
For in each chord, we'll always find,
A soulful bond, forever kind.

## **Playful Clouds Above**

Cotton shapes in skies so blue,
Drifting softly, dreams come true.
Whispers of wind, secrets shared,
Imagination blooms, unprepared.

Chasing shadows, laughter spills,
Over hills and quiet hills.
Children giggle, pointing high,
At the dancing clouds, floating by.

Sunbeams pierce the fluffy white,
In their glow, the day feels bright.
Painting stories for us to see,
In the sky, wild and free.

Let us play beneath their sway,
In this moment, come what may.
For playful clouds will always show,
The joy that life can freely grow.

## Memories That Sparkle

In twilight's glow, we share our dreams,
Whispers of laughter dance in streams.
Colors of joy in moments unfold,
Stories of youth, treasures untold.

Photographs fade, yet hearts remain,
Echoes of love through joy and pain.
Each memory shines, a guiding star,
Illuminating who we are.

The sands of time may shift and sway,
But those bright sparks are here to stay.
In shadows cast by the setting sun,
Every memory's a battle won.

Together we weave our tapestry,
In every thread, a memory.
Shared laughter glimmers, bright and free,
A treasure trove of unity.

# The Symphony of Glee

In a world where laughter reigns,
Joyful hearts break all the chains.
Notes of happiness fill the air,
Creating moments, sweet and rare.

Tap your feet to the rhythm of fun,
Under the glowing, radiant sun.
Dance through life, let spirits soar,
Each moment cherished, forevermore.

Harmony hums in every smile,
Bringing bliss that lasts a while.
Voices mingling, a cheerful cheer,
In this symphony, we hold dear.

Join the song that never ends,
United in joy with all our friends.
As laughter swells and hearts ignite,
A melody of pure delight.

**Tides of Joyfulness**

Waves of laughter crash ashore,
Carrying dreams that we adore.
Each tide brings a brand-new chance,
To wade in joy, to sing, to dance.

Sunrise colors paint the sea,
A vibrant world, wild and free.
As every wave rolls into view,
It whispers secrets, fresh and new.

Seagulls glide on breezy flight,
Their cries harmonize with delight.
With every splash, worries fade,
In nature's rhythm, joy is made.

Let the tides wash over you,
Embracing the waves, a love so true.
Ride the currents, chase the foam,
In joy's embrace, we find our home.

# A Canvas of Light

Brushstrokes horizon, vivid and bright,
Painting the dawn with colors of light.
Each hue a whisper, a tale to tell,
Of moments cherished that fit us well.

Stars sprinkle dreams upon the night,
Illuminating shadows with their light.
In quiet corners, magic grows,
A masterpiece of life that glows.

The sun dips low, casting long rays,
As we weave through the twilight haze.
With each sunset, our stories blend,
Artistry in every curve and bend.

Canvas of life, endlessly wide,
Each stroke a journey, a joy to ride.
In every heartbeat, colors play,
Creating our legacy, day by day.

## **Whirlwinds of Wonder**

Whirlwinds dance in the sky,
Colors twirl as they fly,
Whispers of magic unfold,
Tales of the brave and the bold.

Mysteries swirl in the breeze,
Nature sings with such ease,
Each gust brings a new surprise,
Awakening curious eyes.

In the chaos, joy we find,
Wonders of every kind,
Children laugh, hearts ignite,
Chasing dreams into the night.

Let the whirlwinds take control,
Embrace the magic, be whole,
For in every spin and twist,
Lies a world that can't be missed.

## The Rhythm of Radiance

Morning breaks with golden light,
Birds take flight, hearts feel bright,
Nature's heartbeat, a gentle sound,
In its cadence, joy is found.

Sunlight dances on the leaves,
Whispers through the swaying eaves,
Each ray paints a vibrant scene,
In the warmth, we feel serene.

The dawn chorus starts to sing,
Praises to the coming spring,
In the rhythm, life aligns,
Beauty found in simple signs.

With every beat, we will sway,
In radiance, we'll find our way,
Together, we'll embrace the glow,
Let our spirits freely flow.

**Paths of Delight**

Winding trails through the trees,
Step by step, we find our ease,
Every turn, a view so grand,
Nature holds our wandering hand.

Flowers bloom on either side,
Colors bright, a joyful guide,
With every footfall, laughter spills,
Adventure calls from distant hills.

Gathering moments, sweet and true,
In this dance, me and you,
Paths of life, both old and new,
Leading us to skies so blue.

Hand in hand, we roam in light,
Finding magic in the night,
On these paths, our hearts take flight,
In the journey, pure delight.

**Sparrows in the Sunshine**

Tiny sparrows flit and play,
Glimmers of gold, they sway,
Dancing in the afternoon,
Singing sweetly, a joyous tune.

Each gentle chirp fills the air,
Sunshine smiles with tender care,
As they hop from branch to branch,
In the light, they take their chance.

With wings spread wide, they soar,
Through the skies, forevermore,
In their freedom, we find peace,
Happiness that will not cease.

Sparrows in the day's embrace,
Nature's charm, a warm trace,
In their flight, we too aspire,
To lift our hearts and rise higher.

## The Language of Laughter

Laughter echoes in the air,
A melody beyond compare,
Each chuckle, a vibrant note,
Spreading joy, as hearts float.

In simple moments, smiles ignite,
Turning shadows into light,
With every giggle, warmth expands,
Connecting us, hand in hand.

Laughter, a universal tongue,
Bridges built, old and young,
In its rhythm, worries cease,
A language spoken with such ease.

So let us laugh, both near and far,
A radiant glow, our guiding star,
For in each laugh, a bond we weave,
A joyful tapestry we believe.

## The Dance of Delight

In fields of gold, the sun shines down,
As flowers sway, adorned in crown,
The breeze invites, soft and light,
To join the dance, hearts take flight.

Footsteps follow the rhythm's call,
Joyful laughter weaves through all,
Each twirl and turn, a sparkling cheer,
In the dance of delight, we gather near.

With arms outstretched, we leap and glide,
Casting aside the world outside,
Lost in the moment, time stands still,
Our spirits soar, with zest, with thrill.

So dance with me, in the evening glow,
Let worries fade, let happiness grow,
In every sway and every cheer,
The dance of delight, forever dear.

## Festive Harmonies

The bells chime loud, a joyful sound,
In every heart, good cheer is found,
Voices blend, a sweet refrain,
A chorus of love that will remain.

Colors twinkle, lights aglow,
In festive rhythms, spirits flow,
Gathered friends in laughter unite,
Creating memories, pure delight.

Songs of joy fill every space,
As we embrace this warm, sweet grace,
Hand in hand, we celebrate,
Festive harmonies, a cherished fate.

With every note, our hopes arise,
In this moment, magic lies,
A symphony of joy and cheer,
In our hearts, this love held dear.

## A Sprinkle of Positivity

In morning light, a new day breaks,
With hope in hearts, the world awakes,
A sprinkle of joy, like morning dew,
Brightening life in every hue.

Challenges come, but we stand tall,
With positive thoughts, we conquer all,
Every setback, a chance to grow,
With belief in ourselves, we glow.

Sharing kindness, a gentle touch,
Lifting others, it means so much,
With every smile, we spread the light,
A sprinkle of joy, shining bright.

So let us choose this path today,
In every word, in every way,
A sprinkle of positivity, our creed,
In unity, let love take the lead.

# **Radiant Whispers**

In the garden where blooms sway,
Soft whispers dance on petals' edge.
Colors blend in bright array,
Nature's tales, forever pledge.

Golden rays through leaves will weave,
Secrets shared with every breeze.
In the heart, they softly cleave,
Radiant whispers, gentle tease.

Morning light breaks through the night,
Each moment painted, pure delight.
In the warmth, our dreams take flight,
Guided by the dawn's first light.

Memories in soft embrace,
Laughter caught in whispered song.
In this timeless, sacred space,
Where we know that we belong.

## **Sunlight Serenade**

Underneath the sky so blue,
Sunlight warms the waking earth.
Every ray a promise true,
Filling hearts with joy and mirth.

Gentle breezes sway the trees,
Nature hums a sweet refrain.
Birds are dancing with the leaves,
In this joyful, bright domain.

With each note the sun bestows,
Harmony in every shade.
Life within the stillness flows,
As the world begins to fade.

Embraced by the golden glow,
We find peace in every stride.
In this serenade, we know,
Together, on this journey wide.

## Laughter in the Breeze

In the fields where daisies grow,
Laughter tumbles in the air.
Children's joy in every flow,
Chasing dreams without a care.

Clouds above like cotton sweet,
Fluffy, drifting without bounds.
Every heart, a rhythmic beat,
In this symphony resounds.

Windswept hair and sunny smiles,
Nature's magic all around.
Time is measured in the miles,
Where our laughter can be found.

With the breeze, our spirits soar,
We find bliss in simple things.
In this dance, forevermore,
Life is light as joy takes wing.

**Joyful Echoes**

In the valley, shadows play,
Echoes of a sunlit song.
Memories that drift and sway,
Holding tight where we belong.

Every laugh a spark ignites,
Rippling through the silent space.
In the quiet, pure delights,
Stories shared and hearts embrace.

As the stars light up the night,
Whispers blend with every glance.
In this moment, pure and bright,
Life's a fleeting, magical dance.

Holding hands, we walk as one,
Through the echoes of the past.
In the glow of night's begun,
We find joy that will hold fast.

## **Whirling Dervishes of Delight**

In circles spun with grace and glee,
The dancers twirl, wild and free.
Their skirts a dance of joy and light,
In every spin, the heart takes flight.

The world around a blur of sound,
In motion's arms, bliss is found.
With every whirl, they grasp the sky,
In the moment, time stands by.

When laughter mingles with their tread,
Each joyful tear, a word unsaid.
In unity, both dream and strive,
In each embrace, they come alive.

Through sacred dance, they find their peace,
In twirling steps, all worries cease.
With open hearts and spirits bright,
They are the whirling dervishes of delight.

## The Color of Euphoria

A splash of blue, a dash of gold,
In every hue, stories unfold.
The canvas of a joyful mind,
Where warmth and wonder intertwine.

Violet dreams and emerald smiles,
As laughter paints the world in styles.
With every stroke, hearts come alive,
In vibrant tones, we learn to thrive.

Orange sunsets blend with pinks,
In colors bright, the spirit winks.
Through rainbow paths, we wander wide,
In every shade, the truth won't hide.

Euphoria found in every tint,
A masterpiece where hearts imprint.
In every glance and gentle cheer,
The color of joy, forever near.

## Tapestry of Grins

Threads of laughter and joy entwine,
In a tapestry, so divine.
Each grin a patch, each smile a seam,
Woven together, a vivid dream.

The fabric of friendship, rich and bold,
Stories shared, secrets told.
Stitches bright with memories spun,
In every hue, the joy is won.

From gentle whispers to giggles loud,
In this creation, we feel proud.
Every moment, a vibrant thread,
In this tapestry, love is spread.

A cozy quilt against the chill,
With every grin, our hearts can fill.
In warm embrace, we shall begin,
To share our lives, this tapestry of grins.

## Melodies of Merriment

A tune that dances through the air,
Bringing joy beyond compare.
With every note, the heart takes flight,
In melodies that spark delight.

The laughter echoes, sweet and clear,
As friends unite, and spirits cheer.
Rhythms pulse, a vibrant beat,
In joyous tunes, our lives complete.

Each harmony a tale to tell,
In every sound, a magic spell.
With each refrain, we sway and sing,
These melodies of joy we bring.

In every heart, a song will dwell,
A timeless echo, casting a spell.
Together we craft, both near and far,
These melodies of merriment are our stars.

Milton Keynes UK
Ingram Content Group UK Ltd.
UKHW051811101024
449294UK00007BA/56